IN FLAMES

AURAH POETRY

COVER ILLUSTRATED BY

ANDI GREGORY

IN FLAMES

ISBN: 9781069177100

for those of you who have ever
felt the burn that love can
leave

feel through the fire

then nurse your wounds here

Give yourself some grace in this period of loss. Let your heart sink to your core. Let the memories flow through the flood gates and drown your soul. Let yourself feel and bleed and cry and write. Let yourself mourn for what could have been- for what was supposed to be. For all the promises and plans that were dreamed up in your world together. You need to feel it all. You're a soul who loves so deeply. Who forgives more easily than most. A spirit who fights battles for those they love while fighting your own silent battles inside. You come back bruised and battered but you don't give up. And that's something to admire. It hurts because it mattered. It mattered deeply in every vein that runs through you. It opened you up and made a safe place within you, and you called it home. You gave yourself and your sacred love into hands that weren't always kind. Hands you thought would protect, fight and honor your heart. You shared your power and used it to help them heal, and they left regardless. You're going to feel that in your bones. In every molecule. In every atom.

But make no mistake, my love- it was you who held the flame. It was the fire in you that made the world around you so bright. It was your spark that lit the kindling and roared deep into the night. It was your flame that kept them warm.

The fire is you.

I lie awake at night in a panic

i'm afraid i'll never love anyone like i loved you

like i still love you

i'm fearful it won't be as fulfilling

that even if i do manage to fall in love again there will still be a part of me that's disheartened that it's not you i stand across from at my wedding

that my chest will split in two every time i look at my future children who are half me and half a stranger

who isn't you

i'm terrified that you feel this way too but we're so corrupted that fixing this isn't even possible

one day we will breathe our last breaths earthside

and my final thoughts will *still be of you*

Forever didn't seem long enough for all the life we had planned

to catch all the butterflies that swarmed around us

to feel all that love

now the seconds tick by with every painful throb of my chest

and the time lethargically

grievously

passes without you

I thought i'd always be your sun

your breakthrough beam of light after the rain

the warmth that filled your insides and turned your face towards the sky

your highest focal point and the very thing that got you out of bed in the morning

I believe after time i became too bright

my warmth turned into burns on your too fragile skin

and so you bolt the windows and turned away from my rays

(some people need to live in the shadows)

On nights such as this

there aren't many words for the agony that swells
inside me

the salt soaks my cheeks as the words i cannot seem to
string together claw up my throat

i'm beginning to learn that some catastrophes cannot
be explained or understood

they can only be felt

to stare at the ruins that were once an ever-blooming
garden is a scene i will never recover from

I step back inside the gallery that was once us. I attempt to uncover secrets within the canvas. To study the path which derailed our future. To find reasons or lessons as to why the greatest love I've ever experienced abruptly came to an end. To try and find a space where all this lost love left behind can creep back into my bones and make a home. I torture myself daily. Memories come in waves and it's not long before I am drowning. On occasion, I stop myself before I scrutinize every detail.

Would it make it easier if I had all the answers?

At the end of it all, you're still not here.

We didn't trudge through the hurt and make it through together. We came out wounded, bloodied, with blame on our hands. The chaos came between us when we swore we'd fight together.

I restrain myself.

I list all the reasons how letting go can heal the wounds

that were created.

I clean the salt and dirt from my gashes and find a way to breathe

I try.

I try.

I swear I try.

And maybe tomorrow there'll be victory

I scan each room I enter

check the temperature of the crowd after every display of affection

I research before travelling

to make sure I won't be jailed if i go

because loving who you love is still a crime in

sixty-seven nations

I inspect people's faces after they hear me say the word *"partner"*

as if that word was reserved for *people like us*

I wonder how many aspects of my life would be

different

easier somehow if i loved who they wanted me to love

and yet they still have the nerve to ask

why straight people don't have a fucking parade too

You did not love me like I loved you
your love was nonchalant
and selfish
my love for you was as deep as the ocean
and as predictable as the moon

-your ever changing phases

You didn't reach out on her birthday

she's five today

and it makes me wonder if you ever loved this little human as much as you said you did

if so, how could you not say happy birthday?

or even acknowledge it in the slightest?

did you think of her today?

I'm aware of how i put distance between you two

I didn't want her to feel that inconsistency

my therapist asks, "than why do you let the inconsistency happen to you?"

I reflect on this time last year

when you broke up with me over a phone call at 2am after a night of drinking with your friends

the night before my daughter's birthday party

and all this hurt makes me question the love you claimed to have for either of us

I keep thinking of the night at that little arcade downtown.

Things were turbulent between us, but we were desperate to feel connected again.

There were drinks had and lights flashing, and I'll never forget the way you looked at me across the air hockey table

the way you always looked at me

As if your body was filled with an abundance of desire that turned your eyes to honey. I made every excuse to inch closer. To laugh a little longer. To hold your gaze.

The air between us was buzzing and I needed you.

Things had felt unbalanced for so long that I just *needed you*

We kissed in a bricked doorway down the dark street.

We breathlessly lost track of time and pulled at each other. Desperate. It felt as though we bridged the distance we created. Our bodies and souls sighed a breath of relief

"finally"

And we melted into one. That feeling lingered when your lips were on mine. When your hands were on my face. When you'd smile at me between kisses.

god I loved when you did that

I'd do anything to get lost with you again

The panic gnaws at my insides
turning my reality into a distortion
my heart races and the voices around me muffle
i can feel every atom inside my body telling me to
RUN
that danger lurks like a salivating lion
and i'm the wounded prey
i need out
i need air
i need something
ANYTHING
to take away this fear
i dart into the forest with no relief
i stand as small as an ant in front
of the ocean
but this feels too *all-consuming*
i cage myself inside four walls praying for comfort
i'll sell my soul to never feel this way again
but the vicious beast stalks
looms-and its name is PANIC

How can I feel so

h e a v y

yet so

e m p t y

all at once?

My vision of fate became blurred as i clung to her

a grounding anchor of comfort in a sea of someone else's rocky waves

an unwavering flow of support and ease during a time of pure destruction

devastation

addiction

she showed me how love isn't meant to make you feel small

how love is supposed to hold space for your emotions and feelings

no matter how many ripples of insecurity creep my mind's shoreline

We did this in a past life

many lives i believe

we meet each other time and time again

an instant magnetic pull

we are whisked back into a storm of passion and fire
with a deep knowing that we are meant for one
another

and we try

hard

and we love

harder

forcing the uncomfortable parts of each other to
transform into higher versions of ourselves

we swear it will work this time

but the stars have a different plan don't they

they whisper *"not yet"*

and rip you from my grasp

for now i will learn

and i will grow

and i promise to find you in every life after

"I'm sorry i became someone you had to heal from"

so heal me now

fix these broken parts you created inside me

put an end to this battle inside my mind

ping ponging back and forth about the haunting fact
that you knew

and just couldn't

wouldn't

change

I still believe fate brought you to me
that the universe had some master plan
even though the world ripped us apart

Were you expecting me to stay away this time?

i think my strength caught you off guard

do you believe i'll cave and reach out, desperate for you?

i hold myself back, not letting the world see the emotions fighting viciously inside me

i swear i'm inches away from the edge before i pull it all back

and every time i don't fall back to you

one breath would send me back over the cliff

At times the metaphoric tape across my mouth
threatens to release

i've been struggling with needing to say so much

but saying so little

never before have i felt so much yet stayed so *silent*

In the after

skin to skin blazing

cradled into your arm

breathlessly beating against each other

fingertips connecting the space between the freckles
on your skin

it's impossible to think two people can feel so much

but here we are

your little "i love you" grin pulling at the corners of
your mouth

you're staring at a forest of deep green and honey
while i'm swimming in the jade blue ocean of your
eyes

here is my home

-afterglow

I wonder if you still look up at the crescent of the moon

or gaze at her beauty when she's full

and think of me

does it gather the secrets i've told and whisper them back into your ear?

can you feel the sadness i've poured into it?

night after night

while i beg to be released, to move on

do you stand under the moon and plead for me to wait?

is that why i'm still here?

Not receiving a handmade card from you on my birthday

this is how I know the little things meant the most

The greatest heartbreak comes when they prove they can live without you

even when they promised

swore

vowed

that they never could

It's fine

but that fire that once burned inside me has diminished to embers that weigh heavy in my chest

it's fine

but the sunsets aren't as bright and the ocean isn't as blue and there aren't as many stars at night

it's fine

but i don't see my family as much or my friends all that often and the skies are bewildered in my absence

it's fine

but it's not you

Stop the debate

stop the back-and-forth doubts in your mind

have me fully

messy

wholeheartedly

or don't have me at all

My mind often wanders back to the first of it all. How we spoke constantly over thirty-six hours. I reminisce about the strings that grew between us with every thread of similarity. I go back to the second day when I met you in person and we aimlessly drove around for five hours. Talking. Laughing. I now ache over the end of that night. How you asked to hug me. And how I asked to kiss you. Before the words met the air, your lips were on mine. I remember the girl I was then. How scared she was to fall, knowing there was no halting it. Over the course of just a week, I became so certain that you were the other half of my soul, and we were meant to be here at this exact moment. I craved your presence. I needed to breathe your air. I needed you. A world couldn't possibly exist without us having each other. I think back to believing that no matter where life took us, no matter what happened, we'd always have our world. Everything I did or thought or felt was better simply because you were a part of it. I remember thanking the universe and the moon with every ounce of my being for bringing us together. That fate brought you to me. That this love was bigger than us. That I finally received the love I deserved and somehow that person mirrored how I felt. Memories swell inside me and take my breath away. For now, I'll sit here with the good. With the incredible. With the fireworks and with the hope. I'll pretend. Right now I have to. Right now *I need to believe that you're still here.*

I ponder night and day until i've convinced myself of
the answers

do you regret leaving?

was there anything i could have done to make you
stay?

do you think of me when others touch your skin?

are you better off without me in your life?

did you speak the truth when you made those
promises in the dark?

are you hurting?

I convince myself that there is no possible way you're
mourning like i am

but of course you are, it was undeniably real

and now i'm back to wondering again

-manic cycles

I waited a lifetime to have the love that people write about.

to have captured the type of love i could write about

that many don't even get to experience in their human form

the thing is, once you find it you're not supposed to lose it

and it's not supposed to *leave you*

I count and recount the days until you are home

for your friend's wedding

for good

i fear that the distance is making you drift from me

pulling you into a life that seems brighter without me
in it

as the weeks pass the burning doesn't subside

there's only you and then after you

and i'm stuck in this painful reality

of memories

of lost love

of grieving someone *who's still alive*

I realize that's why this has been so terribly harsh this time

not only did i lose someone i love

i lost a part of me i really loved too

the part of me who fell so incredibly hard

who loved even harder

who believed true love could conquer the world

and heal all wounds

-the princess didn't get her fairytale

At least you were able to escape to the other side of the country where our memories don't linger like stale smoke

Right in front of my bedroom window, leaning against my dresser, is where you asked me to bc yours

This park is where i picked you up and our story began

You played and laughed with my daughter countless times on these swings

We walked these beaches hand in hand finding treasures the ocean offered to us while talking about our pasts

We scoured this island for hidden adventures

We made promises under these stars

You held me at my worst in this house i felt trapped in

With every shift of my eyes i'm suffocated by us

And you were able to open your world up to new places

And mountains that filtered fresh air into your lungs

A fresh slate untarnished by me

Terrified of the worst

so i made the worst happen

worried myself sick thinking about the hurt that
would inevitably come

(or so i thought)

my defenses then created a world of scenarios

bulldozing the foundation before my thoughts became
a reality of ruins

sabotaged it all just to save the devastation

that may never have come

-a powerful mind of insecurities

I don't regret a single second believing you were meant for me

You were here last night in my dream

You came back, asking what took us so long

Your face was in front of mine

Our hearts were beating in the same room

You came back

I woke confused and distorted

Blinking away what i thought was reality

Finally you came back

Now I lie awake, cursing a moment that wasn't real to begin with

Mouring a memory that didn't exist

Nursing another wound on my already pained body

mind

heart

soul

adding another layer of you i now need to miss

I don’t know how to convince myself

that all these parts of me

aren’t half of you

-soulmates

People have been asking me on dates.

"We can go to ponyboat and have a drink, play some arcade games"

"How about we grab some dinner after work?"

"Have you ever been to that café where you can order poporn and play boardgames?"

I can't tell them how I still see you in all these places.

That all I see is us

e v e r y w h e r e

I go

The nervousness during our first date. Playing that stupid mind reader game. Staying until the café closed. The buzzing of the arcade around us and all we could focus on was how close we were to each other. The dinners where we ate and laughed and celebrated. Playfully competitive at mini golf and bowling. All those times we planned

dates for each other, all those surprises. I wanted to make all your dreams come true.

One date at a time.

One step closer to forever, all the way down to *"what's your favorite color?"*

I don't want new memories with strangers. I want more memories with you.

I wanted a lifetime of dates with you

I used to swat in self-defense at vultures who pecked
their way into my life

who swarmed my psyche and made nests within my
body

Vicious men who gawked and called and took away
my right to say no

Cruel creatures who fed off my light in hopes of filling
an addiction or void or mommy issues they never
healed from

Entities that clawed their way into my conscious only
to tear me apart

bit by bit

Those pitiful creatures hide within their shaded trees
now

Still huddling for warmth in a never-ending winter
that is their life

In awe of the phoenix they once called prey

The dread of acceptance pulls my spirit down

like gravity clambering at what once was

they're not coming back for you

they did not love you as fiercely as you loved them

What good is it now, to clutch all this love in my tired hands?

to dissect every moment

trying to soothe my screaming chest

"it doesn't matter now"

The memory grips me, yelling back into the phone

voice hoarse, spirit splitting

"IT DOES MATTER, IT WILL ALWAYS MATTER"

A memory of how i fought

Begged

S h a t t e r e d and even now unrequited love *it still matters*

A sense of calm covers me like a warm blanket now

Where urgency and obsession once restrained me

A new confidence in myself begins to bloom

I will be okay

No matter the outcome

I've studied and rewired the harmful parts inside of myself

And I'll continue to do so

To build a foundation of worth

To stop making others my home

So I will still have roots

No matter the storm

When you bare your soul on pages

and they don't appreciate the narrative

-if you wanted nicer things said about you, you should have been more nice

Anger and hurt swarm my stomach like a colony of distressed bees

you filled my veins with warm silky honey only to retract

and leave me empty nested again

Love isn't supposed to hurt over

and over

and *over*

again

I showed up with an open heart

forgiveness in my hands

willing to start a new path on a broken road

only to be left alone

standing in the destruction that is you

I call back all the power of mine you held in your palms like quicksand

letting precious grains and fragments of me fall to the ground

lost

with no regret or remorse on your end

I call back those delicate parts that you tossed around aimlessly

And this time, i'll put myself back together

That's the thing about someone so in love with words

they hold weight

value

meaning

and you believe them when they're said by someone who promised to hold your heart delicately

but not everyone speaks with the intent of forever

and not everyone has a heart like yours

Strike a match

Rekindle the fire

Only to leave me **in flames**

Those things they did to you

That is not love

Repeat

Repeat

Repeat

The hurt feels different

(more hollow somehow)

when the hope is gone

I almost wish I were back in the thick of aching for you every night

I could almost feel you, even in the silence

my hands bloodied from the grip i had on you

now you've left for the last time

it needs to be the last time

the space between us unrepairable

My limp body lays ripped in half

torn between the always that you promised

and accepting the reality of you not being able to follow through

I arrived at a roadblock in my path where
long walks
deep breaths
and benzodiazepines
couldn't calm my racing mind and trembling hands
Where
self-sabotage
self-harm
and self-deprecating verbiage became my normalcy
A battle with
myself
that i was convinced i could not win
I packed up my alphabet list of diagnoses and fought
hand in hand with
myself
for
myself
not against her
and now we're starting to win
-a forever battle worth fighting

It’s still unfathomable

even after you’ve begged the skies for relief, for them to come back

it still ignites your entire nervous system

sends you plummeting into a world of make belief

It’s something you never thought would happen, even though something within your core always said it would

Are you coming back to me?

or just passing through to make sure our love still has me in a chokehold?

I'm scared to risk having to say goodbye again

What if I'm the same me

And you're the same

You

The plunge my heart takes when your lips crash to mine could sink the tallest of ships

bring rushed flowing rivers to deserts

could set galaxies ablaze

star by star

we stop time

nothing else matters

all i hear is the thump of your heart against mine

finally finally finally

"We will always support you, I guess we just don't understand it"

As if someone's gender or identity was theirs to *understand*

As if seeing me beam for the first time in years was hard to *understand*

How the wind was knocked out of my lungs for days after that conversation

And how i pledged to spend the rest of my relationship

the rest of my life

standing up for someone i love so they never feel misunderstood in my presence

-you're safe here

Maybe we had to heal what was

to make room for what could be

Is it possible to make peace upon ruins?
to grow trust and love again, where ashes lay?
to turn the page
or rather start a new book entirely
and in this tale
we may finally make it

Time may have passed

distance separated us

but our souls were always *here*

Your body curves into mine like the sliver of a
crescent moon

our fingers inner-twined

our lazy breaths matching

with each exhale i become less of me

and more of us

This is what it feels like to be two halves of one soul

You'll never be able to forget what my love felt like

-a vengeful promise

After months of waiting in a comatose state

i deserved more than it to end in

"I shouldn't have reached out"

I am not a choice for you to regret

I am not a third-place priority

I am not a body you use to feel something

I am a soul that you never deserved in the first place

Staggered beliefs were imbedded in my skin

Ones that told me love was measured by how hard you fought for someone

How much you compromised and suffered

A purer life is teaching me that love is persistence

Stability

how unhealthy obsession is not love

but how calm love is supposed to be

how love is supposed to show up

e v e r y t i m e

The lost love looms over me like a dark, heavy cloud

I'm petrified that i'll never look at anyone else and think

forever

I’m missing you regardless

maybe i could have done the distance after all

-would i still have you if i tried harder?

I sit and convince myself that it wasn't all for nothing

That i grew

That i challenged the darkest parts of my spirit

and filled them with light

I tell myself that i was lucky enough to have had the opportunity to experience an all-consuming type of love

Although now i'm starting to believe that what you don't know can't hurt you

and what you don't feel *you can't miss*

I hope you get everything you've ever wanted, and it **still isn't enough**

No one tells you how to come alive again after love
imploded on your heart like a live wire

No one tells you how empty you'll feel after the
electricity is gone

You built all these worlds up outside of us

bricks made of my unconditional love and support

pieces of me that you stole

In lieu of your selfish empire

i was left drained

and you sat on your thrown and watched me dissipate

I cannot continue to crawl back to someone who doesn't even want to stay

-merry go round love

You've abandoned where you used to call home
You've emptied the carcass that housed your heart
And now I board the windows shut and lock up tight
They'll be no trespassing here

Healing the mind and heart after someone broke you in two

is its own type of *superpower*

I was made to feel

crazy

invalidated

over-emotional

disposable

and still begged for you to love me

"please i'll do anything"

She puts her little hand in mine and reminds me every day that love is *real* and love is *here*

-luckiest mama alive

Love-bombing

passion

affection

sex

REWARD

cold

condescending

unpredictable

cruel

PUNISHMENT

-the highs and lows of you

The loss of you pulls my body down like an anchor today

reminding my soul that we're not free of you yet

Why did you promise me the depths of the ocean

only to take it all away with the changing tide?

How does it feel to be my greatest regret

when you could have continued to be

the love of my life?

Trying to recreate all those perfect memories and feelings

over and over

even after the hurt

even after all the disrespect

-the avoidant and the anxiously attached

Trying to medicate the pain with the very person who caused all this hurt

who continues to cause hurt

-loving a narcissist

Just get over it

they weren't meant for you

move on

you deserve better

just *let it go*

But let it go where?

nowhere could fit all this hurt

And these people don't understand the chokehold a trauma bond can have

they didn't see the love that was shared and how deeply it ran

So i stay silent with my heartbreak

and i pour myself onto these pages

Left and lost in a place where love doesn't exist
anymore

my world is muffled, my edges dull

very little brings me to the surface anymore

I hate who i've become

I have spent more time healing in my life

than i have spent *actually living it*

You learned so much about yourself

but you used me to do it

-human sacrifice

Pinholes were poked into my skies
just enough air to keep me alive
what i really needed was the ocean
and enough breath to fill my lungs
-space

I want to take their hand and keep it here with me

with this mess

"are you still mine?" i'd say

"do you still want this?"

but i stay silent

i couldn't tolerate hearing them say *no*

When they ask you what your favorite moment was

you will say me

you will always say me

and it will choke you on the way out

The sun is beaming behind the blackout curtains

a reality i don't want to face

I imagine the clouds are dark and heavy in a midnight sky

and the moon is engorged

filled with my secrets of you

This is where my sadness comforts me

-I don't want to face sunshine if it's not with you

Connecting with other

minds

bodies

mouths

feels like a foreign unwelcomed zap of electricity

feels like betrayal towards a ghost who still looms and haunts

I pray for sleep to come as your energy pulls at my light

as your gravity sinks me down

across thousands of miles and different time zones

Something deep within our galaxy anchors me here no matter how hard i beg for release

I ask the stars why

but they've been dead for billions of years

and still shine

still have to

And I wonder if that will be my fate too

Tales of how you desperately longed for me fall from your mouth

I eagerly gather them from the ground on bloodied knees and dirty hands

I hold these words to my chest

yearning to feel how i once did

I peel back the abandonment like damaged skin

I nurse the wound to find pieces of debris that must
be tended to

Uncertainty

Betrayal

Shame

of my own doing

nestled deep

And only once they're brought to the surface do i
finally start to heal

-forgive yourself, too

Safety feels like stale air

when you've become so accustomed to chaos

Seasons change and with that comes a new
opportunity to bring you back

meditations and manifestations

spells and herbs and colored wax

full moon intentions written on crumpled paper

wishes on 11:11 and birthday cake candles

It is only once every avenue has been explored does it
dawn on me

Only you can bring yourself back

and if you wanted to

you'd be here

With every milestone and memory you've missed the blade painfully digs in deeper

I store them in my mind like old films

hoping one day i'll play them for you and you'll cry and laugh during all the right moments

Then i clutch my torso and the crimson red blood stains my hands

I look up with confusion

Hot tears streaming down my face

I'm reminded of who put the knife there in the first place

A distortion of who i thought you were fades away

-how much can you possibly bleed for someone?

I built a fortress of protection around the one thing in my body that lives for love

You tore through my armor and presented peace after years of devastation

I called off the troops and ceased the fire

I waved the white flag of surrender

Only for you to attack when I was my most vulnerable self

Alone

Unprotected

And now more wounded than ever before

My lover is a ghost

a figment of my imagination

a memory of a soul i thought i knew

a dream i've had since the beginning of time

My lover is a delusion

A mask with a demon underneath

Her little warm palm cradles my cheek as she falls asleep just after saying she's going to make a card for me at school tomorrow

"Just cause you're so nice to me mama"

My heart swells and my eyes water

as I'm reminded of why I'm still here

of why I was ever here in the first place

I breathe an aura of light around us

Sending an energy of love and abundance her way

She turns over "Your hands are cold mama"

and holds my hand against her beating innocent heart

I may never get love right

I may follow and create destruction wherever I go

But cross my heart

and hope to die

I will not fuck this up

I will not fuck her up

I will never be someone she needs to heal from

The narcissist feeds the addict another syringe of dopamine

take this hit and remember what it was like before

Before your cruelty stonewalled in front of my eyes

Before your silence left me questioning my sanity

Before you twisted reality into a distortion that made me just give in

let this sink into your veins and remind you that you can only feel this way because of me

Leave me weak and hollow for the next dose that inevitably will have me returning for more

A tsunami looms overhead at all times

threatening to spill chaos across my world at any given moment

The slightest inconvenience sending me into a tailspin

and tragedies sending me towards the nearest cliff

It is a curse and a blessing to feel everything so deeply

to take everything to heart like a dagger

to feel like a burden to those around you

To feel so intensely is exhilarating and exhausting all at once

-BPD

The abandonment has rotted my insides

The decay has forced the butterflies to scatter

Here lies the body and mind of a soul whose spirit you drained

without so much as a glance back at my tombstone

yet here you are again

dancing in the graveyard that is us

asking for my hand to begin the waltz we know too well on brown deadened leaves

wondering why my bones have become ridged and cold to the touch

They say to love someone is to let them go

But there's something painfully beautiful about
holding on for *dear life*

Little did you know

all those times you left

slowly taught me how to live without you

jokes on you i can breathe

Take me back to a time

when

you fell in love with the beautiful parts of me

before the darker parts made you love me less

The uneasiness spreads through my body like wildfire

your stern hands hold the match

With flushed cheeks and a jittering chest i ask for reassurance

I'm looked down upon under a puffed-out chest and somber eyes

I am a woman of fierce power within

who's been torn down by your words

forced to become more malleable

easier for you to handle

What will it take to finally make me break?

How much longer could i possibly *burn for you?*

The right one will not try to hush the storms in your mind for their comfort

they'll run to safety with you

protect you

regardless of the forecast

Make yourself smaller

so their ego can fit

It ran in the family

until it crashed into me

Generational behaviors bled down onto innocent beings

And i had the choice

to keep the century old wounds open

or heal them within me

Raised faded scars live on my skin

but my own flesh and blood

(the heart that lives outside of my body)

remains unscathed

And that's the most important thing I'll do in this life

I've gone blue in the face

trying to get you to understand my feelings

searching for a sliver of validation

pleading with your eyes to finally see that switch of light

Just say you're sorry, just admit you were wrong

But the sorrys don't come

and the validation I desire is nowhere in sight

So I take a step back

And I take a bigger breath in

And I pray that I'm finally strong enough to choose myself this time

The person i love leaves your body with the blink of an eye

Cruelty snakes through your veins, on its way to deplete me

Once your god complex takes over, that's it

i am not the love of your life anymore

but in your eyes, i become someone beneath you who couldn't possibly feel for themselves

Venom drips from your mouth

words you cannot take back

Once again you've left another victim poisoned

In some tales there is not a beautiful beginning

a devastating middle

and a sunshine end of inspiration and hope

Some stories are still being written

the hurt lingering a little longer than hoped

Some stories are still messy

the authors continue to mourn and question and fight to grow

Some experiences don't come in pretty little packages

where the final pages symbolize light at the end of a broken-hearted tunnel

some of us are still **in flames**

thriving struggling clawing breathing healing loving hurting breaking growing *all at once*

These pages are here to show you that you're not too much. That your feelings are valid. That there is no timeline or right way to heal.

These pages bare my soul

So you can see that **you're not alone**

Thank you for being here

- aurah poetry

Manufactured by Amazon.ca
Bolton, ON

44275446R00061